Bible ESL
Book 1
Lessons 1-5
Arrival Of The King

Learn English Through the Bible
Harvest Field Publishing
2026

Table of Contents

THE BIRTH OF JESUS

Scan for More

My Lesson Notes

Name: ____

Date: _____________________

My new word: _______________________________________

Notes:

____

____

____

____

____

____

____

____

____

____

____

This Lesson's Bible Reading

Matthew 1:18–25

The birth of Jesus Christ happened like this. Mary was engaged to Joseph, but before they lived together she became pregnant by the Holy Spirit. Joseph was a good man and did not want to shame her, so he planned to send her away quietly. An angel of the Lord appeared to him in a dream and said, "Joseph, do not be afraid to take Mary as your wife. The child is from the Holy Spirit. She will have a son. You will name him Jesus because he will save his people from their sins."

This happened to fulfill what the Lord said through the prophet: "The virgin will have a son, and they will call him Immanuel," meaning God with us.

Joseph obeyed the angel. He took Mary as his wife and named the child Jesus.

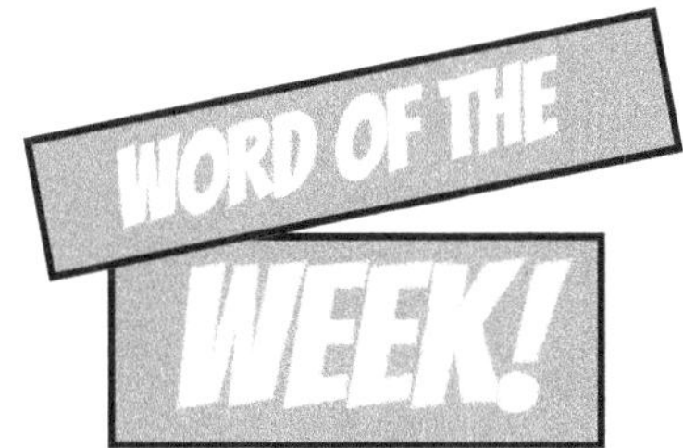

HOPE

BIBLICAL DEFINITION

Hope in the Bible means trusting God and believing He will do what He says. It means believing God will bring good things in His time.

Hope is not just wishing. It is trusting God even when we cannot see what will happen next.

"For I know the plans that I have for you," says God, "plans for your welfare and not for evil, to give you a future and a hope."
- *Jeremiah 29:11*

"Now faith is assurance of things hoped for, proof of things not seen."
- *Hebrews 11:1*

The concept of hope in the Bible has roots in the Jewish tradition where the faithful anticipated the coming of the Messiah. *In the Old Testament*, hope was often linked to waiting for God's deliverance. For example, the Israelites hoped for freedom from slavery in Egypt and later for return from exile. *In the New Testament,* hope is closely tied to the resurrection of Jesus Christ and the promise of eternal life, reflecting the early Christians' anticipation of His second coming.

MODERN DEFINITION

Hope is the feeling that something good can happen. It means believing the future can be better and not giving up.

SYNONYMS:
Faith, Trust, Belief

ANTONYMS:
Fear, Doubt, Hopelessness

MODERN-DAY EXAMPLES

1. Despite problems, she kept hope for better days.

2. He worked hard because he hoped for a better life.

EXERCISE

Try using this word in a sentence and write it below. It can be in a Biblical context or a modern day context.

____

____

____

____

REFLECTION

Hope helps us when life is hard. It helps us trust God when we have problems. When things feel difficult, hope reminds us that God is still working. Each day we can choose to trust Him. God keeps His promises. Because of this, we can live with courage, peace, and joy.

SUPER CHALLENGE

Use the "Word of the Week" at least three times today in a conversation with others. You may write your conversation ideas below.

- ____
- ____
- ____

THE BIRTH OF JESUS

✓ WARM UP: *VOCABULARY BUILDING*

Draw a line to match the word to its correct definition.

Angel   •   • Wrong things people do
Bethlehem   •   • A messenger from God
Sins   •   • Town where Jesus was born

READING COMPREHENSION

1. Read the passage below and **highlight** or circle the vocabulary words given.

After you have finished reading the first time.

2. Read the passage again and underline the words or phrases that are difficult for you.

Mary was going to have a baby. An angel told Joseph not to be afraid. The baby was from God. His name would be Jesus. He would save people from their sins. Jesus was born in Bethlehem. He was a special gift from God.

REFLECT & DISCUSS

Answer the following questions based on the passage read.

1. Where was the baby from?

____

____

2. Where was Jesus born?

____

____

3. Why did God send Jesus?

____

____

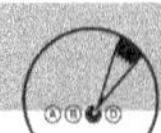 VOCABULARY CHECK

1. Define these words based on your understanding from the passage:

   a. Angel - ____

   b. Bethlehem - ____

   c. Sins - ____

2. Use each of these words in a sentence.

   - ____

   - ____

   - ____

3. Try to find someone you know and explain at least one of these words to them.

QUICK CHECK

Read each question carefully. Circle the letter of the correct answer.

1. **Who told Joseph not to be afraid?**

   a. Mary   b. A King   c. An Angel

2. **Why did God send Jesus?**

   a. To go to school

   b. To rule the land

   c. To save people from their sins

3. **Who gave Jesus to us as a special gift?**

   a. Joseph   b. Angel Gabriel   c. God

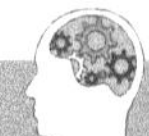 MEMORY VERSE

1. Look for a line from the Gospel story summary.
2. Memorize the chosen line.
3. Practice saying it aloud.
4. Write the verse from memory.
5. Compare it to the original

 **WRITE & DISCUSS**

Write a short paragraph of two to four sentences reflecting on the question below. Write as if you are discussing this with someone close to you. Use the space provided to write down your answer. Use a separate sheet, your journal, or the back of this paper if necessary.

What can we learn from the story of Jesus' birth?

____

____

____

____

____

REFLECTION: *Journaling & Sharing*

Reflect on the story you read. Write down your reflection below or in your journal. You can also share them in class, with friends, or with family.

How does this passage make you feel? How can you apply its lessons to your life?

____

____

____

____

____

LET'S DO MORE!

Welcome to the bonus section of our ESL module, where we dive deeper into the world of English language learning! Here, you'll find exciting activities designed to enhance your language skills beyond the core lessons.

GUESS THE WORD

Each scrambled word below is related to the passage. Use the provided definitions as clues to unscramble the letters and find the correct word. Write your answer in the space provided.

Example: **Not known or seen by others** : s e c r e t l y (lyecsetr)

1. A messenger from God   ______________ (lnega)
2. The town where Jesus was born   ________________ (hmebleeht)
3. Wrong things people do   __________ (sni)

SPEAK UP: *Try your best if you can!*

1. Find a partner to do this activity with.
2. Write a paragraph or two below or in your journal for someone, reflecting your thoughts and experience.

Think about a childhood story, yours or one from your family. Share your story and explain what made it special or memorable.

____

____

____

____

BIBLE THREADS

THE CONNECTION BETWEEN THE OLD AND NEW TESTAMENT THAT REVEALS GOD'S PLAN AND PURPOSE

For the exercises below, refer to the original handout as well as the bonus section.

Read and ponder on the Bible passage on the scroll below and answer / do the activities that follow.

> **"Therefore the Lord himself will give you a sign. Behold, the virgin will conceive, and bear a son, and shall call his name Immanuel."** -Isaiah 7:14

REFLECT & DISCUSS

How can this teaching from the Bible verse or the Bible Threads section help you in your interaction with your family, friends, and community? Write a short paragraph and try to use at least two of the vocabulary words.

____

____

____

____

____

WORD OF THE WEEK

Use the WOW - Word of the Week in a phrase or sentence.

A PRAYER TO GOD

1. Write a short prayer to God, reflecting on the verse above.
2. Write it first in your own language and then in English.

____

____

____

____

____

____

____

____

ANSWERS:

VOCABULARY BUILDING

- Angel - A messenger from God
- Bethlehem - Town where Jesus was born
- Sins - wrong things people do

QUICK CHECK
1. c. An Angel
2. c. To save people from their sins
3. c. God

GUESS THE WORD
1. Angel
2. Bethlehem
3. Sin

Scan for More

BOOK 1

Lesson 2

Bible ESL — Gospel Series
© 2026 Harvest Field Publishing. All rights reserved.

Scripture quotations are from the World English Bible (WEB), a public domain translation.
No permission is required for its use.

No part of this publication may be reproduced, distributed, or transmitted in any form or by any means, including photocopying, recording, or other electronic or mechanical methods, without prior written permission from the publisher, except for brief quotations used in teaching, review, or ministry contexts.

BibleESL.com

Scan for More

My Lesson Notes

Name: ____

Date: ___________________

My new word: ___________________________________

Notes:

This Lesson's Bible Reading

Matthew 2:1–12

Jesus was born in Bethlehem during the time of King Herod. Wise men from the east came to Jerusalem asking, "Where is the one born King of the Jews? We saw his star and came to worship him."

Herod was troubled and asked the priests where the Christ would be born. They said Bethlehem.

Herod told the wise men to find the child and report back. The star led them to the place where Jesus was. They were very happy when they found him.

They bowed down and worshiped him.

They gave him gifts of gold, frankincense, and myrrh.

God warned them in a dream not to return to Herod, so they went home another way.

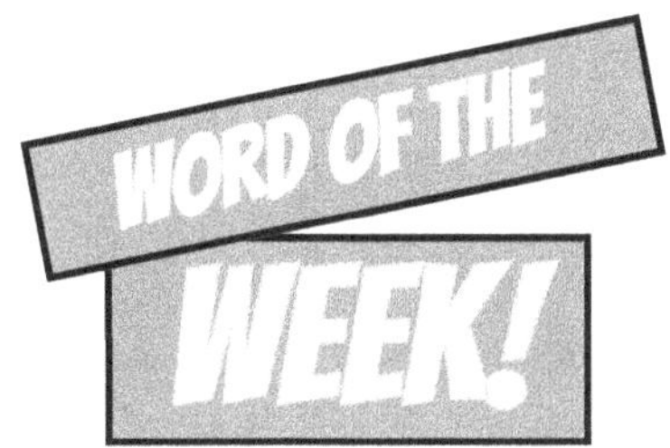

MAGI

BIBLICAL DEFINITION

The Magi were wise men from the East who came to see Jesus after He was born. They followed a special star that led them to Him. They brought gifts of gold, frankincense, and myrrh.
They came to honor Jesus as King.

"Then the king placed Daniel in a high position and lavished many gifts on him. He made him ruler over the entire province of Babylon and placed him in charge of all its wise men."
-Daniel 2: 48

"On coming to the house, they saw the child with his mother Mary, and they bowed down and worshiped him."
- Matthew 2: 11

DID YOU KNOW?

After Jesus was born in Bethlehem, wise men from the East saw a new star. They understood it was a sign that a new king was born. They traveled a long way to find Him. When they found Jesus, they bowed down and gave Him gifts.
God warned them in a dream not to go back to King Herod,
so they went home another way.

MODERN DEFINITION

Magi means wise men. It can describe people who study, learn, and look for truth.

SYNONYMS:
Wise men, Teachers, Scholars

ANTONYMS:
Fools, Ignorant People

MODERN-DAY EXAMPLES

1. The Magi followed the star to find Jesus.

2. The wise men brought gifts to the child.

EXERCISE

Try using this word in a sentence and write it below. It can be in a Biblical context or a modern day context.

____

____

____

____

REFLECTION

The Magi wanted to find Jesus. They were willing to travel far to see Him. They gave their best gifts to honor Him. We can learn from them. We can also look for Jesus and give Him our best. We can honor Him by how we live each day.

SUPER CHALLENGE

Use the "Word of the Week" at least three times today in a conversation with others. You may write your conversation ideas below.

* ____

* ____

* ____

VISIT OF THE MAGI

✓ WARM UP: *VOCABULARY BUILDING*

Draw a line to match the word to its correct definition.

Wise •	• A bright light in the sky
Star •	• To go after someone or something
Followed •	• Having good judgment

READING COMPREHENSION

1. Read the passage below and **highlight** or ⓒircle the vocabulary words given.

After you have finished reading the first time.

2. Read the passage again and underline the words or phrases that are difficult for you.

Wise men saw a star in the sky. They followed it to find baby Jesus. They brought gifts of gold, incense, and myrrh. King Herod was jealous. But the wise men listened to God and did not return to Herod.

REFLECT & DISCUSS

Answer the following questions based on the passage read.

1. What did the wise men follow, and why did they follow it?

____

____

2. What gifts did they bring?

____

____

3. Why didn't they return to Herod?

____

____

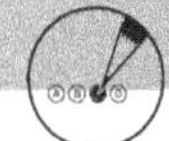 **VOCABULARY CHECK**

1. Define these words based on your understanding from the passage:

   a. Wise - ____

   b. Star - ____

   c. Followed - ____

2. Use each of these words in a sentence.

   - ____

   - ____

   - ____

3. Try to find someone you know and explain at least one of these words to them.

QUICK CHECK

Read each question carefully. Circle the letter of the correct answer.

1. **What did the wise men see?**

   a. A rainbow   b. A star   c. An angel

2. **What gifts did the Magi bring to Jesus?**

   a. Gold, silver, and spices

   b. Jewelry, perfume, and animals

   c. Gold, frankincense, and myrrh

3. **What was King Herod's reaction to the news of Jesus' birth?**

   a. Happiness   b. Jealousy   c. Indifference

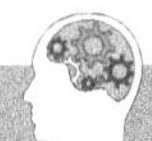 **MEMORY VERSE**

1. Look for a line from the Gospel story summary.
2. Memorize the chosen line.
3. Practice saying it aloud.
4. Write the verse from memory.
5. Compare it to the original

WRITE & DISCUSS

Write a short paragraph of two to four sentences reflecting on the question below. Write as if you are discussing this with someone close to you. Use the space provided to write down your answer. Use a separate sheet, your journal, or the back of this paper if necessary.

What did you learn from the wise men's visit to Jesus?

____

____

____

____

____

REFLECTION: *Journaling & Sharing*

Reflect on the story you read. Write down your reflection below or in your journal. You can also share them in class, with friends, or with family.

How does this passage make you feel? How can you apply its lessons to your life?

____

____

____

____

____

LET'S DO MORE!

Welcome to the bonus section of our ESL module, where we dive deeper into the world of English language learning! Here, you'll find exciting activities designed to enhance your language skills beyond the core lessons.

MATCH THE WORD

Match each definition to the correct vocabulary word from the box provided. Write the vocabulary word next to its corresponding definition.

Wise	Herod	Followed	Star

1. Having good judgment   ________________________
2. A bright light in the sky   ________________________
3. To go after someone or something   ________________________

SHOW AND TELL

Suppose that you are one of the Magi who visited, draw the gift that you would bring to Him in the box below. Write a short explanation as to why you chose this gift.

BIBLE THREADS

THE CONNECTION BETWEEN THE OLD AND NEW TESTAMENT THAT REVEALS GOD'S PLAN AND PURPOSE

For the exercises below, refer to the original handout as well as the bonus section.

Read and ponder on the Bible passage on the scroll below and answer / do the activities that follow.

> **"Nations will come to your light, and kings to the brightness of your dawn."** - Isaiah 60:3

REFLECT & DISCUSS

How does Isaiah 60:3 relate to the visit of the Magi in Matthew 2: 1-12? What does it suggest about Jesus' significance?

____

____

____

____

____

____

WORD OF THE WEEK

Use the WOW - Word of the Week in a phrase or sentence.

A PRAYER TO GOD

1. Write a short prayer to God, reflecting on the verse above.
2. Write it first in your own language and then in English.

ANSWERS:

VOCABULARY BUILDING
- Wise - Having good judgment
- Star - A bright light in the sky
- Followed - To go after someone or something

QUICK CHECK
1. b. A star
2. c. Gold, frankincense, and myrrh
3. b. Jealousy

MATCH THE WORD
1. Wise
2. Star
3. Followed

Scan for More

BOOK 1

Lesson 3

THE ESCAPE TO EGYPT

Bible ESL — Gospel Series
© 2026 Harvest Field Publishing. All rights reserved.

Scripture quotations are from the World English Bible (WEB), a public domain translation.
No permission is required for its use.

No part of this publication may be reproduced, distributed, or transmitted in any form or by any means, including photocopying, recording, or other electronic or mechanical methods, without prior written permission from the publisher, except for brief quotations used in teaching, review, or ministry contexts.

BibleESL.com

Scan for More

My Lesson Notes

Name: ____

Date: _____________________

My new word: _______________________________

Notes:

____

____

____

____

____

____

____

____

____

____

This Lesson's Bible Reading

Matthew 2:13–23

After the wise men left, an angel of the Lord appeared to Joseph in a dream. The angel said, "Get up. Take the young child and his mother, and flee to Egypt. Stay there until I tell you, because Herod will try to kill the child."

Joseph got up during the night and took Jesus and Mary to Egypt. They stayed there until Herod died.

Herod became very angry when he knew the wise men had not returned. He ordered the killing of the young boys in Bethlehem and the nearby area.

After Herod died, an angel appeared to Joseph in Egypt. The angel said, "Get up. Take the young child and his mother, and go to Israel."

Joseph returned, but he was afraid to go to Judea. After being warned in a dream, he went to Galilee and lived in Nazareth.

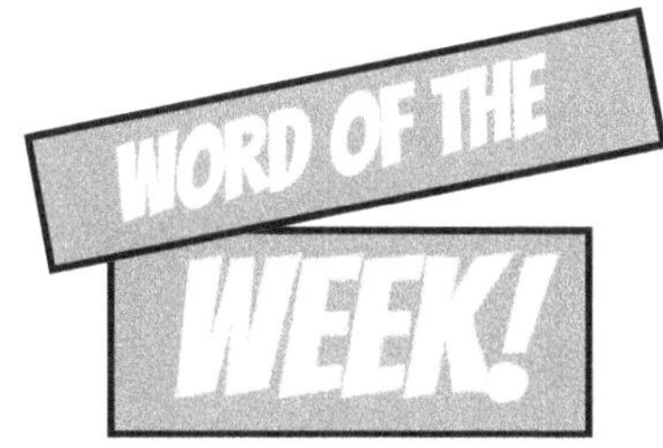

ANGEL

BIBLICAL DEFINITION

An angel is a messenger from God. Angels bring God's messages and help carry out His plans. In the Bible, angels often bring guidance, warnings, or good news.
They remind people that God is with them and watching over them.

"He had a dream in which he saw a stairway resting on the earth, with its top reaching to heaven, and the angels of God were ascending and descending on it."
-*Genesis 28:12*

"Suddenly, an Angel of the Lord appeared and a light shone in the cell. He struck Peter on the side and woke him up, 'Quick, get up!' he said, and the chains fell off Peter's wrists."
- *Acts 12:7*

An angel came to Joseph in a dream. The angel told him not to be afraid to take Mary as his wife. The angel also told him that Jesus would save people from their sins. Later, an angel warned Joseph to take Mary and Jesus to Egypt to stay safe. God used angels to guide and protect them.

MODERN DEFINITION

An angel is a spiritual messenger from God. People also use the word angel to describe someone who is very kind or helpful.

SYNONYMS:
Messenger, Helper, Servant

ANTONYMS:
Enemy, Devil, Evil Spirit

MODERN-DAY EXAMPLES

1. The angel told Joseph what God wanted him to do.

2. She was like an angel because she helped everyone.

EXERCISE

Try using this word in a sentence and write it below. It can be in a Biblical context or a modern day context.

____

____

____

____

REFLECTION

Angels remind us that God cares for His people. God guided Joseph through the message of an angel. God still guides us today through His Word and through wise advice. We can trust God to lead us when we do not know what to do. Like Joseph, we can listen and obey God.

SUPER CHALLENGE

Use the "Word of the Week" at least three times today in a conversation with others. You may write your conversation ideas below.

- ____

- ____

- ____

THE ESCAPE TO EGYPT

✓ WARM UP: *VOCABULARY BUILDING*

Draw a line to match the word to its correct definition.

Angel •   • Did what he was told to do

Egypt •   • A country where Joseph took Jesus

Obeyed •   • A messenger from God

READING COMPREHENSION

1. Read the passage below and **highlight** or (circle) the vocabulary words given.

After you have finished reading the first time.

2. Read the passage again and underline the words or phrases that are difficult for you.

An angel warned Joseph in a dream: "Take Mary and Jesus and go to Egypt." King Herod wanted to hurt Jesus. Joseph obeyed. After Herod died, they came back and lived in Nazareth.

○ REFLECT & DISCUSS

Answer the following questions based on the passage read.

1. What did the angel tell Joseph?

____

____

2. Why did Joseph take his family to Egypt?

____

____

3. Where did they live after Herod died?

____

____

 VOCABULARY CHECK

1. Define these words based on your understanding from the passage:

    a. Angel - _______________________________________

    b. Egypt - _______________________________________

    c. Obeyed - _______________________________________

2. Use each of these words in a sentence.

    • _______________________________________

    • _______________________________________

    • _______________________________________

3. Try to find someone you know and explain at least one of these words to them.

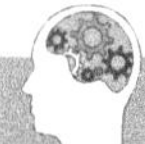 QUICK CHECK

Read each question carefully. Circle the letter of the correct answer.

1. **Who warned Joseph?**

    a. An angel   b. A prophet   c. King Herod

2. **Why did Joseph, Mary, and Jesus have to leave their home?**

    a. Herod wanted to give them a present

    b. Herod wanted to kill Jesus

    c. They wanted a new home

3. **Where did Joseph take Mary and Jesus to escape Herod?**

    a. Bethlehem   b. Jerusalem   c. Egypt

MEMORY VERSE

1. Look for a line from the Gospel story summary.
2. Memorize the chosen line.
3. Practice saying it aloud.
4. Write the verse from memory.
5. Compare it to the original

 WRITE & DISCUSS

Write a short paragraph of two to four sentences reflecting on the question below. Write as if you are discussing this with someone close to you. Use the space provided to write down your answer. Use a separate sheet, your journal, or the back of this paper if necessary.

What can we learn about trusting and obeying God?

____

____

____

____

____

REFLECTION: *Journaling & Sharing*

Reflect on the story you read. Write down your reflection below or in your journal. You can also share them in class, with friends, or with family.

How does this passage make you feel? How can you apply its lessons to your life?

____

____

____

____

____

LET'S DO MORE!

Welcome to the bonus section of our ESL module, where we dive deeper into the world of English language learning! Here, you'll find exciting activities designed to enhance your language skills beyond the core lessons.

 **GUESS THE WORD**

Each scrambled word below is related to the passage. Use the provided definitions as clues to unscramble the letters and find the correct word. Write your answer in the space provided.

Example: **Not known or seen by others** : s e c r e t l y (lyecsetr)

1. A vision or message received during sleep. _ _ _ _ _ (mrade)
2. A messenger of God _ _ _ _ _ (lnega)
3. To go back to a place _ _ _ _ _ _ (rnertu)

 **SPEAK UP:** *Try your best if you can!*

1. Find a partner to do this activity with.
2. Write a paragraph or two below or in your journal for someone, reflecting your thoughts and experience.

Think about a time when you or someone you know had to move to a new place for safety or a better life. Share who moved, why they moved, where they went, and what challenges they faced.

____

____

____

BIBLE THREADS

THE CONNECTION BETWEEN THE OLD AND NEW TESTAMENT THAT REVEALS GOD'S PLAN AND PURPOSE

For the exercises below, refer to the original handout as well as the bonus section.

Read and ponder on the Bible passage on the scroll below and answer / do the activities that follow.

"When Israel was a child, I loved him, and out of Egypt, I called my son." -Hosea 11:1

REFLECT & DISCUSS

How does Hosea 11:1 relate to the events in Matthew 2:13-23?
What does it say about God's plan for Jesus?

____

____

____

____

____

____

WORD OF THE WEEK

Use the WOW - Word of the Week in a phrase or sentence.

A PRAYER TO GOD

1. Write a short prayer to God, reflecting on the verse above.
2. Write it first in your own language and then in English.

ANSWERS:

VOCABULARY BUILDING

- Angel - a messenger from God
- Egypt - a country where Joseph took Jesus
- Obeyed - Did what he was told to do

QUICK CHECK

1. a. An angel
2. b. Herod wanted to kill Jesus
3. c. Egypt

GUESS THE WORD

1. dream
2. angel
3. return

Scan for More

BOOK 1
Lesson 4

Scan for More

My Lesson Notes

Name: ____

Date: ___________________

My new word: _________________________________

Notes:

____

____

____

____

____

____

____

____

____

____

____

This Lesson's Bible Reading

Matthew 3:13–17

Jesus came to John the Baptist at the Jordan River to be baptized.

John tried to stop him and said he needed Jesus to baptize him.

Jesus said it was right to do this to fulfill righteousness, so John baptized him.

When Jesus came up from the water, heaven opened. The Spirit of God came down like a dove and rested on him.

A voice from heaven said, "This is my beloved Son.

I am very pleased with Him."

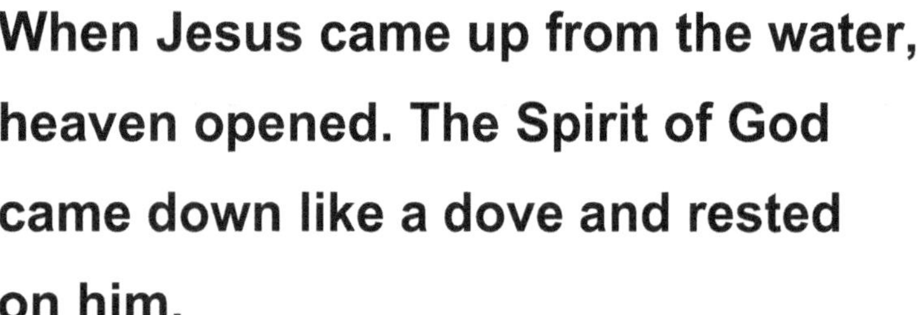

WORD OF THE WEEK!

BAPTISM

BIBLICAL DEFINITION

Baptism is a special act that shows a person wants to follow God. In the Bible, baptism often uses water. It shows a new beginning and a changed life. Jesus was baptized to show obedience to God and to begin His public work.

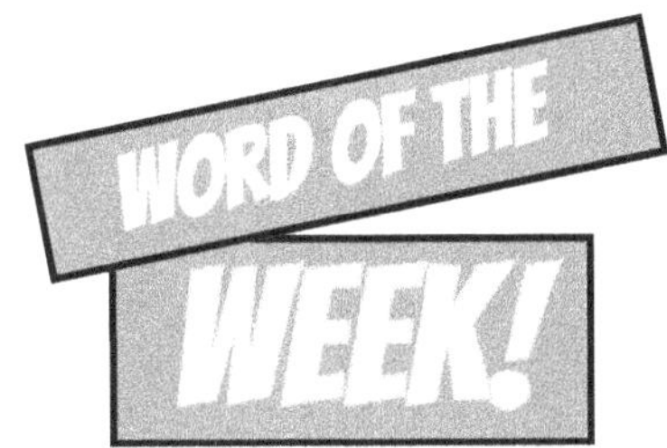

"Encourages the cleansing and washing away of sins."
-Isaiah 1:16

"Repent and be baptized."
 Acts 2:38

John the Baptist baptized people in the Jordan River. He called people to turn away from sin and follow God. When Jesus came to John, John was surprised and felt unworthy. But Jesus said it was right to do this. When Jesus was baptized, the Holy Spirit came down like a dove, and God said Jesus was His Son.

MODERN DEFINITION

Baptism is a church ceremony using water. It shows a person's faith and their decision to follow Jesus.

SYNONYMS:
Washing, Cleansing, Beginning

ANTONYMS:
Sin, Disobedience

MODERN-DAY EXAMPLES

1. He was baptized to show his faith in Jesus.

2. Baptism showed her new start with God.

EXERCISE

Try using this word in a sentence and write it below. It can be in a Biblical context or a modern day context.

____

____

____

____

REFLECTION

Jesus chose to be baptized even though He had no sin. He showed obedience to God. Baptism reminds us that following God is a choice. It also reminds us that God sees our faith. Each day we can choose to follow Jesus by how we live, speak, and treat others.

SUPER CHALLENGE

Use the "Word of the Week" at least three times today in a conversation with others. You may write your conversation ideas below.

- ____

- ____

- ____

THE BAPTISM OF JESUS

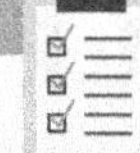

✓ WARM UP: *VOCABULARY BUILDING*

Draw a line to match the word to its correct definition.

Repent •   • A white bird symbolizing peace

Baptize •   • To feel sorry for sins

Dove •   • To put someone in water for God

READING COMPREHENSION

1. Read the passage below and **highlight** or circle the vocabulary words given.

After you have finished reading the first time.

2. Read the passage again and underline the words or phrases that are difficult for you.

John was a man who told people to repent. He baptized people in the river. One day, Jesus came to be baptized. As Jesus came out of the water, God's Spirit came down like a dove. A voice from heaven said, "This is my Son."

REFLECT & DISCUSS

Answer the following questions based on the passage read.

1. What did John tell people to do?

____

____

2. Who came to be baptized?

____

____

3. "What did the dove show about Jesus?"

____

____

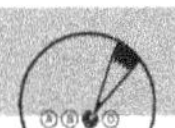 VOCABULARY CHECK

1. Define these words based on your understanding from the passage:

   a. Repent - ____

   b. Baptize - ____

   c. Dove - ____

2. Use each of these words in a sentence.

   • ____

   • ____

   • ____

3. Try to find someone you know and explain at least one of these words to them.

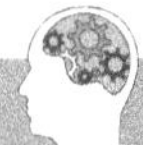 QUICK CHECK

Read each question carefully. Circle the letter of the correct answer.

1. **Who baptized Jesus?**

   a. Peter   b. John the Baptist   c. Moses

2. **What did the voice from heaven say during Jesus' baptism?**

   a. "This is my beloved Son."

   b. "Behold the Lamb of God."

   c. "Peace be with you."

3. **What came down from heaven as Jesus was baptized?**

   a. Fire   b. An angel   c. A dove

MEMORY VERSE

1. Look for a line from the Gospel story summary.
2. Memorize the chosen line.
3. Practice saying it aloud.
4. Write the verse from memory.
5. Compare it to the original

WRITE & DISCUSS

Write a short paragraph of two to four sentences reflecting on the question below. Write as if you are discussing this with someone close to you. Use the space provided to write down your answer. Use a separate sheet, your journal, or the back of this paper if necessary.

Why is Jesus' baptism story important?

____

____

____

____

____

REFLECTION: *Journaling & Sharing*

Reflect on the story you read. Write down your reflection below or in your journal. You can also share them in class, with friends, or with family.

How does this passage make you feel? How can you apply its lessons to your life?

____

____

____

____

____

LET'S DO MORE!

Welcome to the bonus section of our ESL module, where we dive deeper into the world of English language learning! Here, you'll find exciting activities designed to enhance your language skills beyond the core lessons.

MATCH THE WORD

Match each definition to the correct vocabulary word from the box provided. Write the vocabulary word next to its corresponding definition.

Preach	Confess	Dove	Heaven

1. To admit one's sins. ______________________
2. To deliver a religious message. ______________________
3. A white bird symbolizing peace. ______________________

SPEAK UP: *Try your best if you can!*

1. Find a partner to do this activity with.
2. Write a paragraph or two below or in your journal for someone, reflecting your thoughts and experience.

What does baptism mean to you? How can it help you follow God better?

____

____

____

____

BIBLE THREADS

THE CONNECTION BETWEEN THE OLD AND NEW TESTAMENT THAT REVEALS GOD'S PLAN AND PURPOSE

For the exercises below, refer to the original handout as well as the bonus section.

Read and ponder on the Bible passage on the scroll below and answer / do the activities that follow.

> **"A voice of one calling: 'In the wilderness, prepare the way for the Lord.'"** -Isaiah 40:3

REFLECT & DISCUSS

How does Isaiah's prophecy about preparing the way relate to John the Baptist's mission and the coming of Jesus in Matthew 3:13-17?

____

____

____

____

____

____

WORD OF THE WEEK

Use the WOW - Word of the Week in a phrase or sentence.

A PRAYER TO GOD

1. Write a short prayer to God, reflecting on the verse above.
2. Write it first in your own language and then in English.

____

____

____

____

____

____

____

____

ANSWERS:

VOCABULARY BUILDING

- Repent - to feel sorry for sins
- Baptize - to put someone in water for God
- Dove - a white bird symbolizing peace

QUICK CHECK
1. b. John the Baptist
2. a. "This is my Son."
3. c. A dove

MATCH THE WORD
1. Confess
2. Preach
3. Heaven

Scan for More

Lesson 5

THE TEMPTATION OF JESUS

Scan for More

My Lesson Notes

Name: ____

Date: ___________________

My new word: _______________________________________

Notes:

____

____

____

____

____

____

____

____

____

____

____

This Lesson's Bible Reading

Matthew 4:1–11

Jesus was led into the wilderness to be tempted by the devil. After fasting forty days, he was hungry.

The devil said, "If you are the Son of God, turn these stones into bread."

Jesus answered, "Man shall not live by bread alone but by every word from God."

The devil tested him again, but Jesus answered with Scripture each time.

Finally Jesus said, "Worship the Lord your God and serve him only."

Then the devil left him, and angels came to help him.

TEMPTATION

BIBLICAL DEFINITION

Temptation is when someone feels pulled to do something wrong. In the Bible, Jesus was tempted by Satan in the wilderness. Jesus did not sin. He answered each temptation with God's Word and stayed faithful to God.

"The temptation of Eve in the Garden of Eden."
-*Genesis 3:6*

"Explain how temptation arises from one's desires."
- *James 1:14*

After Jesus was baptized, He went into the wilderness for forty days. During this time He did not eat. Satan came and tried to tempt Him. Satan told Jesus to turn stones into bread and to test God's protection. Jesus refused. He trusted God and used Scripture to answer each test.

MODERN DEFINITION

Temptation is the desire to do something we know is wrong or not wise.

SYNONYMS:
Test, Pull, Desire

ANTONYMS:
Obedience, Self-Control

MODERN-DAY EXAMPLES

1. He felt temptation to cheat but chose honesty.

2. She avoided temptation by making a better choice.

EXERCISE

Try using this word in a sentence and write it below. It can be in a Biblical context or a modern day context.

____

____

____

____

REFLECTION

Everyone faces temptation. Jesus showed us how to respond. He trusted God and used Scripture. When we face temptation, we can also choose what is right. We can pray, remember God's Word, and make good choices. God gives us strength to say no to wrong things.

SUPER CHALLENGE

Use the "Word of the Week" at least three times today in a conversation with others. You may write your conversation ideas below.

- ____

- ____

- ____

THE TEMPTATION OF JESUS

✓ WARM UP: *VOCABULARY BUILDING*

Draw a line to match the word to its correct definition.

Wilderness   •   • To try to make someone do wrong

Tempt   •   • Food made from flour and water

Bread   •   • A place with no people or food

READING COMPREHENSION

1. Read the passage below and **highlight** or (circle) the vocabulary words given.

After you have finished reading the first time.

2. Read the passage again and underline the words or phrases that are difficult for you.

Jesus went into the wilderness for 40 days. He did not eat. The devil came to tempt Him. He told Jesus to turn stones into bread. But Jesus said, "Man does not live on bread alone." Jesus did not give in to temptation.

REFLECT & DISCUSS

Answer the following questions based on the passage read.

1. Where did Jesus go for 40 days?

____

____

2. What did the devil want Jesus to do?

____

____

3. What did Jesus say about the bread?

____

____

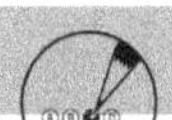 VOCABULARY CHECK

1. Define these words based on your understanding from the passage:

   a. Wilderness - ____

   b. Tempt - ____

   c. Bread - ____

2. Use each of these words in a sentence.

   - ____

   - ____

   - ____

3. Try to find someone you know and explain at least one of these words to them.

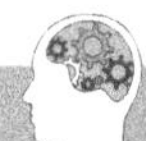 QUICK CHECK

Read each question carefully. Circle the letter of the correct answer.

1. **Who tempted Jesus in the wilderness?**

   a. the Devil   b. An angel   c. Moses

2. **What did Jesus say about living by bread alone?**

   a. Man does not live by bread alone.

   b. "Behold, the Lamb of God."

   c. It is necessary.

3. **How long did Jesus fast?**

   a. 20 days   b. 30 days   c. 40 days

MEMORY VERSE

1. Look for a line from the Gospel story summary.
2. Memorize the chosen line.
3. Practice saying it aloud.
4. Write the verse from memory.
5. Compare it to the original

WRITE & DISCUSS

Write a short paragraph of two to four sentences reflecting on the question below. Write as if you are discussing this with someone close to you. Use the space provided to write down your answer. Use a separate sheet, your journal, or the back of this paper if necessary.

How can we apply Jesus' responses to temptation in our daily lives?

____

____

____

____

REFLECTION: *Journaling & Sharing*

Reflect on the story you read. Write down your reflection below or in your journal. You can also share them in class, with friends, or with family.

How does this passage make you feel? How can you apply its lessons to your life?

____

____

____

____

____

LET'S DO MORE!

Welcome to the bonus section of our ESL module, where we dive deeper into the world of English language learning! Here, you'll find exciting activities designed to enhance your language skills beyond the core lessons.

MATCH THE WORD

Read each sentence carefully. Identify the correct word that matches the definition in the underlined phrase in each sentences. Underline the correct answer.

> **Example:**
> He was **enticed** to eat the cake, even though he knew that he was not allowed.
> <u>a. Tempted</u>   b. Excited   c. Afraid   d. Refused

1. **Some people deliberately <u>go without food for a period of time</u> as their practice.**

   a. Fast   b. Feast   c. Eat

2. **We hiked for hours through <u>a wild place with no people or food.</u>**

   a. Buildings   b. Wilderness   c. Island

3. **She felt a <u>strong desire to do something not good</u> for her health.**

   a. Temptation   b. Say   c. Think

SPEAK UP: *Try your best if you can!*

1. Find a partner to do this activity with.
2. Write a paragraph or two below or in your journal for someone, reflecting your thoughts and experience.

What strategies can you use to overcome temptations in your life?

____

____

BIBLE THREADS

THE CONNECTION BETWEEN THE OLD AND NEW TESTAMENT THAT REVEALS GOD'S PLAN AND PURPOSE

For the exercises below, refer to the original handout as well as the bonus section.

Read and ponder on the Bible passage on the scroll below and answer / do the activities that follow.

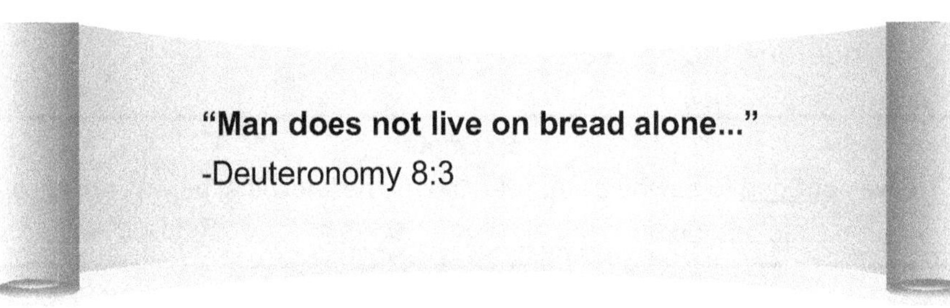

REFLECT & DISCUSS

How does the teaching in Deuteronomy about relying on God's word relate to Jesus' response to the Devil's temptations in Matthew 4: 1-11?

____

____

____

____

____

____

WORD OF THE WEEK

Use the WOW - Word of the Week in a phrase or sentence.

A PRAYER TO GOD

1. Write a short prayer to God, reflecting on the verse above.
2. Write it first in your own language and then in English.

____

____

____

____

____

____

____

____

ANSWERS:

VOCABULARY BUILDING
- Wilderness - A place with no people or food
- Tempt -To try to make someone do wrong
- Bread - Food made from flour and water

QUICK CHECK
1. a. the Devil
2. a. It is not enough.
3. c. 40 days

MATCH THE WORD
1. a. Fast
2. b. Wilderness
3. a. Temptation

Scan for More

About the Author

Christopher Smith is the creator of Bible ESL, a structured English learning system built around clear, accurate Bible texts. He has years of experience teaching, writing, and developing practical learning tools designed to help students grow in both language skill and confidence.

Bible ESL was created to make English accessible through meaningful content. Each lesson focuses on clarity, structure, and steady progress, helping learners improve vocabulary, comprehension, and communication skills step by step.

Christopher develops all materials with a focus on simplicity, accuracy, and real-world usability.

May God bless you as you continue to grow in your understanding, your faith, and your confidence in English. May His Word guide your learning and strengthen you each day.